The Road 1 Readability :
Basics of writing and editing

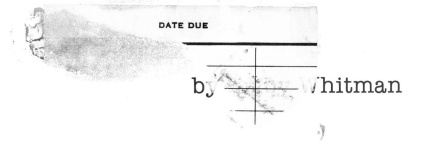

by _____ Whitman

Lawrence Ragan Communications, Inc.
CHICAGO

Ragan Books, Chicago 60610

© 1993 by Digby Butler Whitman
All rights reserved. Published 1993
Printed in the United States of America

93 94 95 96 97 98   11 10 9 8 7

Lawrence Ragan Communications, Inc.
212 W. Superior Street
Chicago, Illinois 60610

ISBN   0-931368-17-0

Contents

Part three   Gracenotes

FOR ELEANOR
Without whom I'd be neither
an editor or a writer, but
a beachcomber.

Foreword

Digby Whitman: Apologist for Craftspersonship

To write about writing in a newsletter on writing for people whose jobs demand expertise in writing is to stand naked before your peers. Among the writing consultants whose copy it has been my pleasure to edit for the *Ragan Report*—Alden Wood, Peter Jacobi, Edmund Arnold, Larry Ragan—Digby Whitman occupies a place of special affection and admiration.

For many years Digby directed communications for Employers of Wausau. The advice on writing, editing, photography, layout, headlines, and editorial balance that Digby presents here are the fruits of years of careful husbandry in organizational communications. I've never regretted taking his advice. It comes from an uncommonly rich experience.

Part of that experience is Digby's willingness to take risks, both verbal and social. His conservative counsel in a well-publicized debate on sexist language in the January 18, 1982, *Ragan Report* was full of humor: "I think that any writer who deliberately commits singular-plural error to avoid sexist construction is out of their mind.'' In this case, the risk was to side with prescriptive grammar. The debate ended with Digby admitting, ''All I want is ERA and a quiet life.''

His best columns on writing always involve that sense of social efficacy. His recent attacks on the supermarket press—''I SOLD MY BABY TO UFO ALIENS''—express a simultaneous outrage at bad writing and socially irresponsible ''journalism.''

His January, 1981, *Ragan Report* column on irresponsible reporting of the Iranian hostage crisis—and the likelihood that the returning hostages would, themselves, become participants in the instant celebrity press—was reprinted in the Op-Ed page of the *New York Times.*

So in Digby's emphasis on good writing, we see a man who views good writing, clear thinking, and responsible behavior as inseparable.

Digby's insistence on civilized—even elegant—writing is what makes him stand out from most commentators on the language. The letters of Walt Whitman's great-nephew are passed around our office immediately upon their arrival. No two close the same: ''Hastily but indignantly''; ''Don't eat yellow snow''; ''Time to lubricate''; ''If there is anything corporate communicators hate it is corporate counsel.''

They are valued for their humor, both playful: ''Here's a nessay''; and elegant, as this opening upon the recovery of his dog: ''Let sound the loud timbrel o'er Egypt's dark sea: Boomer seems to be convalescing successfully.''

They are valued for their wealth of literary allusions—to Shakespeare, Chesterton, Johnson, the Bible. ''Stevenson, like several others, is my favorite writer.'' ''Who praised the majestic justice of the law, which, with utter impartiality, forbids rich and poor alike to sleep under bridges?''

The verbal risks that emerge from being too well-read sometimes lead Digby into murky waters. In the fall of 1982, he described the tendency of annual reports to substitute glossy exteriors for substance, thereby neutering their impact, as ''gelding the lily.'' We got letters.

But though prescriptive, Digby is not insensitive. In response to a letter in which the word "referenced" was used several times, Digby writes: "That I have overlooked this indecency and written him politely testifies, I think, to the tolerance I have acquired in my old age."

Elegant writing as a mark of civil tolerance is one of Digby's identifying characteristics. Modern organizational communicators, beset on all sides by the new technology and by pressures to see their jobs as "managing issues" may well ask why we need another book on writing and editing well. Digby's answer—in this book and, implicitly, in the topics and style of his own writing—is that we need now to strive more than ever toward civility, in the workplace and in our own jobs.—**Patrick Williams**

Part One

Physics and mechanics

1

Objectives and priorities

Let's take a few minutes to get our ducks in a row. How would you, as an editor-writer, answer this question: "What is the first purpose of your journal?"

In the light of workshop experience, if your vehicle is aimed at your customers or stockholders or the general public, I should expect you to stress your company's image—the value of its goods or services, the soundness of its stocks, its overall integrity. If your enterprise is a hospital, utility, or has other special claims to public support, you'll probably concentrate on creating a climate favorable to fund drives or bond issues or legislation in your employer's interest.

If it's an employee publication you'll describe objectives such as high morale, operational economies, employee identification with your company's goals and objectives, pride of craft and service, career paths—everything that adds up to the message: "This is a good company to work for!"

Since editors and writers are by habit and practice both

literate and articulate, your reply will be both intelligent and well-worded.

Nine times in ten, it will also be wrong.

The *first* purpose of any written communication—cookbook, love letter, matchbook cover, skywriting, sonnet, whatever—is to be *read.* You will almost certainly have skipped right past that one to dwell on your organization's purpose in publishing the journal at all. But those purposes must be listed second and third and fourth and so on down the line.

Please don't dismiss this as wordplay or smart-alecry. No matter how lofty and laudable a publication's aims may be, they cannot be realized unless and until that first purpose has been achieved. The history of journalism is littered with the corpses of once-great magazines and newspapers whose editors lost sight of that rule. And conversely, no publication that has succeeded in that vital first purpose has ever failed to prosper, regardless how tawdry or corrupt or completely without merit its ideals and goals.

Of course this doesn't mean that the editor of an organization's publication has no more to do than achieve readability and readership. That may be enough for periodicals whose profits are measured in dollars and derived from subscriptions and newsstand sales. You are in different case.

Which brings up an interesting point. Your management may not be aware that the job they have given you is ultimately much tougher than those of the people whose names adorn the mastheads of *Saturday Review, Newsweek, Hustler,* and the rest of the commercial press. For them, that first step is the last step. For you, it is only the vital preliminary to *motivating* your readers, not just informing or diverting them. You too seek a profit, but its nature is such that it cannot be recouped unless your journal is not only read, but responded to and acted upon. As long as the buyer of any commercial publication keeps on reading it, its publishers and editors don't care what he does after he puts it down. You *do* care.

But that comes later. The second purpose of the present paper—the *second* purpose—is to help you accomplish, for yours, the first.

2

First things first

"I don't know where to begin," said Alice.

"Begin at the beginning," suggested Humpty-Dumpty, "go on until you come to the end, and then stop."

Following that sage advice, we'll begin with your cover.

Pause for a minute or two in front of the next sizeable newsstand you pass. Notice how the periodicals are competing, almost visibly jostling one another for your attention. Flamboyant flesh, intellectual stimulus, romance, adventure, the latest styles—the promises vary from journal to journal, but the message is the same: "Look inside me!"

Your publication must compete with all of these. When you place it in the hands of your readers, you are asking them to give it equal or superior attention to these periodicals—not to mention books, theater marquees, television, or that evening's sunset. Yet, as I flip through the stacks of publications on the card table beside me, most of their covers are dismayingly alike. They run to dense clouds of type, crowded margins, faces peering dimly from too-small photographs too often indifferently reproduced.

There are pleasant exceptions, and there is nothing to prevent you from making yours one of them. Begin with this principle: *The only function of your cover page is to arouse interest in those that follow.*

Does a picture of your workplace or its grounds do this? Probably not. Does a studio photograph of its president, or a posed group shot of its board of directors, do it? Positively not. A spectacularly good color photograph of almost anything may indeed nail attention to the cover, but it does little to draw the viewer inside. Besides, good color photography costs money, and you are more interested in attention-getters that don't strain your budget.

The surest way to beckon readers past your cover is to let it give them a tantalizing glimpse of what they'll find behind it. An arresting example: the five words "I'm dead—see page 12" on the cover of *hi-points*, published by Loveland Instruments Div., Hewlett Packard Co. (Gregg Piburn, Editor, P.O. Box 301, Loveland, CO 80537).

What top management changes may mean for you.

If you get sick, how much will you have to pay?

What are your chances of becoming an alcoholic?

No; I've never seen any of those banners; I offer them only as the kind of bait I'd rise to. Splashed across supporting illustration, or run in stark black typeface over blank white stock, such headlines transform your cover from a shut door to an inviting entryport into your publication.

Of course this won't work, or at least it won't work for long, unless your publication's contents keep its cover's promises. That's the subject of our next section.

3

Editorial balance and selection

Employee publications

What you print in your publication is a reflection of what you are as an organization. It's surprising how alike vastly different organizations' publications are: column after grey column of people celebrating anniversaries; announcements of births, marriages, deaths; and the wide-column messages from the CEO or chairman that no one reads from start to finish. It's clear that editors learn by imitating, which ends up perpetuating the same old, bad habits.

You may argue that those announcements reflect the people of your organization; that it's your job to give them that type of recognition. But most of the people in the organization won't recognize the face, the name, the date. Who reads those announcements with any interest except the person in it, his family, her friends?

True, we do like to read *about* people. And an employee publication should be *for* and *about* employees. But it should be more than a simple list. It's like those "mug-shots" lined up across the page: they show what a person *looks* like, not what a person *is* like. Every organization is filled with people celebrating anniversaries, births, marriages, promotions. Communicating the events in that manner does nothing to help its employees define the character of the organization they work for. How can employees help carry out the organization's goals if they can't define the organization or its goals?

A Few stand for many

We can define our organization and its goals by presenting them *through* the employees in our publications. Then we're saying something about the place and its people. Instead of running those tiny pictures of solemn faces, run a few big pictures that say something about the people in the picture. Do an interview of a few of the people celebrating anniversaries. Let them tell why they've stayed with the organization for 10 or 25 or 30 years. What do they remember about the organization when they started? What differences have key changes made in their jobs over the years? What might they have done differently? When you write about benefits *show* don't *tell* why they're called benefits. Focus on one or two specific cases and then let the employee tell, as much as possible, in his or her own words, how the benefit worked. Don't ignore the facts, but show how the facts apply. Let a few instances represent many instances. We each read and use the information most useful to us—but it has to be in useable form for us to even try to get it.

The Proactive communicator

We sometimes confuse our jobs with the job of the commercial press. We want to report everything that happens, just like Dan Rather or Connie Chung. The problem is that by the time the story is written, pasted-up, printed, and distributed in our monthly publications, the hot news is cold. Everybody knows it already. Why bother?

There's good reason to bother, even with the old news, as Roger D'Aprix makes clear in his book, *Communicating for Productivity,* (from which we've borrowed heavily in writing this section), because there's something we do that no other publication can do for employees of our organizations: we can motivate them to help the organization flourish by helping them identify with it. And that includes telling what happened, even when everybody already knows what happened. More than that—and we fail if we don't take it this far—we also tell *why* it happened and what it means for employees. That's good organizational communication. It answers basic questions: "How will the changes in upper-management affect me?" "Will I be laid off because my division had a bad year?" "What are our organization's priorities and goals and how do I fit in?" "Will anyone listen to my suggestions for doing the job better?" That's called *pro*active communication. It helps bridge gaps.

You need cooperation from management to perform this kind of communication, but proactive communications programs *demand* closer ties with management. You are their mouthpiece in a way that serves the employees: like a telephone receiver rather than a megaphone. It's communication that goes both ways. By staying aware of employees' needs and questions you can get answers from management for them. You assist management by helping employees define their roles in the organization and the organization's role in the community. And that will help employees plan their futures with your organization. It gives them reasons to stay and reasons to work.

Once this function is understood and accepted, it cannot be successfully performed by the personnel department in its spare time. It's a full-time job for someone whose sole responsibility is to motivate employees by identifying and presenting the goals of the organization to them. You need not be a professionally experienced editor or writer to begin with. Intelligence and literacy beget professionalism. You *do* need superiors—and budget-setters—who share your sense of your publication's mission.

4

Photography, artwork, layout

A picture can advance a story. It can tell a story. In very rare and memorable instances, it can even *be* a story. Let's look at artwork in that order.

The first category is that of illustration. Here the photo or drawing explains and illuminates the printed text. Used relevantly, it contributes both clarity and economy to the message. A square-inch sketch can describe a corkscrew more eloquently than a page of verbal exposition.

In category No. 2 these places are reversed. Pictures carry the story, with word-function confined to the briefest possible captions. Here again, however, relevance must be maintained. An idea is being communicated, and the business of the photograph or artwork is to clarify and advance it.

In its third and loveliest role the picture comes into its own. Here one could say that relevance is irrelevant. A sunrise, a kitten, surf, the smile on the face of a child, or dew on the face of a flower—these glimpses are of themselves complete. Captions just get in the way. But even if you are lucky enough to come by such treasures, I must

16

regretfully recommend against using them on the front cover of your publication, which, as noted earlier, should function as an entryport to the inside pages. The picture for its own sake belongs on your back cover or inside back cover. It's a reward.

The Tussaud touch

In one of Rex Stout's whodunits Archie Goodwin, the "I" of the stories, apostrophizes on the human ego. "If the National Chairman of one of the major political parties should phone you tonight to tell you his party wants to run you for the Presidency of the United States," says Archie, "of course you'd act surprised. But you wouldn't really *be* surprised."

This may be an inch or two exaggerated. But most people are very easily convinced that their pictures would adorn and improve any printed text. This is probably why, in so many business publications, the most frequent use of the camera is for its most sterile function: the posed snapshot or portrait. People are shown shaking hands with each other, pointing out objects to each other, giving awards and plaques to each other. Faces peer dimly from tiny headshots. Grounds for new construction are broken by executives wearing hard hats over Ivy League suits, holding shovels as if they were canoe paddles.

I know this stuff is expected of you; I've been in your shoes. Probably you don't like it any better than I do, but feel you can't altogether get away from it. But get away as far as you can. The least interesting aspect of humanity, and the most depressing, is what it looks like. Not appearance, but action is the proper subject of the camera. Photograph people, sure, but show them busy, working, playing, making things happen. And the happening, not the people, should dominate the picture.

If you must run portraits, and I suppose you must, insist on good ones and give them the room they deserve. More than four to a page is too many. Crowded banks of inch-square head-and-necktie shots, posed groups of boards of trustees looking as if they had just stepped from Madame Tussaud's Waxworks Gallery—don't clog your pages with them.

Above all, never admit grimy or light-struck or badly-cropped photographs to your magazine. Murky photography should be excluded as rigorously, and for the same reasons, as murky prose. Blank space is better.

Artwork

Pen or pencil sketches, cartoons, or even stick-drawings offer agreeable variants to camera shots. They can add the touch of humor so badly needed—and so usually wanting—to enliven narrative exposition. This kind of thing is readily and cheaply available from the commercial cutbooks.

Layout and design

Most business journals, and nearly all low-budget media of any kind, are afflicted by one common defect: that of overload. If your publication runs on a tight budget (and most do) the chances are that you are struggling with more cargo than your vehicle should really be carrying.

Let's suppose that an expert like Ed Arnold or Jan White should advise you to choose between two courses. Either add 20 per cent to your present bulk—i.e.: if you are running eight pages go to ten; if 16 go to 20—without any increase of text, or if you can't afford that, jettison 20 per cent of your present text while keeping the same number of pages. You would almost certainly protest that neither choice is acceptable. You haven't room now for material you'd like to print. Your restricted budget both precludes adding more pages and constrains you to pack those you have to the last inch.

Very understandable. But very bad economics.

Skimpy margins, columns squeezed cheek to jowl, too-

small or inadequately leaded typefaces, are paid for in the
vital currency of lost readership. The message may all be
aboard, but that's where much of it will stay. It won't be
delivered. There is no surer way to waste space—and
money—than to carry cargo that never leaves the hold.

Air, space, light, are requisites for effective layout and
design.

Color me black on white

Color is so regularly misused in organizational print media
that I am sometimes tempted to congratulate editors who
have to do without it. Not having it can keep them out of
several different kinds of trouble. But color can
be a blessing when employed properly—which means, first
of all, sparingly.

Vertical or horizontal colored dividers, preferably on
white surfaces, can add a sprightly touch to a page. Colored
stock for covers or wraparounds is fine, especially if it can
be varied from issue to issue, distinguishing each from the
last. For inside pages it's riskier, and should be confined to
light and cheerful pastels. Colored print on colored stock is
frequently a mistake. Colored print run across colored
photography is almost inevitably disastrous.

Caxton (or was it Gutenberg?) invented the printing press
500 years ago. From that day to this, the easiest print to
read has always been the blackest possible ink on the whitest
possible surface. If you can't hold yourself back from an
occasional splash of colored type on a colored surface
purely for the sake of elegance, go ahead; nobody's perfect.
But you will be buying elegance and spending legibility.

Your best friend in all these matters of journalistic
architecture is a skillful and imaginative printer. If you are
fortunate enough to have such a source, draw on it to the
fullest. If you aren't, keep looking until you find one. Good
printers and good editors make good partners.

Part Two

Writing and editing

5

Perspective, ambience, and stuff

So far, we have been tinkering with the physics and dimensions of your publication. In moving into its actual writing and editing, we are going not from one kind of work to another, but from work to fun. Writing has a lot in common with childbirth. It can be excruciating, but it is rewarded by satisfactions as pure and undiluted as any to be found in a naughty world.

Please don't think of what follows as a classroom exercise. I'm not your teacher; I'm your host. We are a couple of writing editors, sitting before my fireplace (if it's winter) or out on my patio (if it's summer). We are engaged in a level and lateral conversation. The conversation must perforce begin as a monologue, because that's the way print travels. But what is offered is not dicta, but opinion. And if I'm doing all the talking while you are doing the listening, this booklet will close with an invitation for you to talk back. We just might keep the conversation going for years.

May I freshen your drink? Fine. We're off!

6

Words at work:
The CIPP code

If I owe the United States Post Office nothing else (and I can't think of much else offhand) I am indebted to it for a reminder device that I recommend to every writer and editor.

To accomplish its purpose, your message must a) be understood, b) command attention, c) *sell* the reader, and d) stay in his mind. These elements may be neatly packaged in four key words whose initial letters compose what I use as my CIPP Code:

- Clarity
- Impact
- Persuasiveness
- Penetration

All four are as vital to the successful operation of your newsletter as are four wheels to the successful operation of an automobile. A communication may be perfectly clear and yet make no dent on the reader's mind. It may be forceful without being convincing. It may be persuasive, but soon forgotten. If even one of the four qualities is lacking, the message stalls or loses its way. Effective writing may be defined as writing that puts them all to work, and keeps them working *together*. Let's take them separately.

7

Words at work:
Clarity

Prose clutter is the greatest single enemy of prose clarity.
There are as many kinds of clutter as there are of weeds.
Most have their hardiest life in business and political writing
and speechifying, but two especially morbid growths can trip
any but the most wary writer or editor.

The first is clutter by redundancy. The last and most
dreadful legacy of Watergate, threatening to linger in our
speech long after the speakers' names have been forgotten,
is "at this point in time" for "now" and "at that point in
time" for "then." But surely nobody, not even a politician,
could sink into language as diseased as that without having
sickened toward it on a diet of such lesser offenses as these:

The Long Way Round	The Short Way Home
accompanied by	with
answered in the negative	said no
at the present time	now
experience has indicated that	I have found

it is to be assumed that	I suppose
it is our opinion that	we think
it is possible that we might	we may
meets with our approval	we like it
reasonable facsimile	good copy
subsequent to	after

The list could be extended—indeed, you might want to keep and fatten it. Watching for this kind of dreary word wastage in other peoples' copy is a good way of keeping it out of your own.

A second common contributor to clutter is tautology. You wouldn't write or say "a round circle." But are you proof against all of these?

> basic fundamentals
> cirrhosis of the liver
> consensus of opinion
> free gift
> new innovation
> self-addressed envelope
> self-conceit
> self-confessed
> true facts
> unconfirmed rumor
> unproved suspicion
> unvarnished candor
> widow woman
> yellow jaundice

Those modifiers do about as much for their nouns as barnacles do for a boat. All facts are true. All widows are women. No envelope ever addressed itself—what's wrong with "reply envelope"? Cirrhosis, by definition, is a disease of the liver, and "jaundice" *means* yellow.

Even commoner and more catching is clutter by strangulation. But since this destroys impact rather than clarity, it is deferred to the next section.

8

Words at work:
Impact

A word, a phrase, a paragraph, or an essay delivers impact in exactly the same way as does an arrow or a bullet—by going directly to its target with all possible velocity and momentum. Or more precisely, by being *propelled* to its target.

One way to demonstrate clutter by strangulation is to take unstrangled prose and strangle it. Winston Churchill began his great Dunkirk speech with the words: "The news from France is very bad." He closed it just as simply: "With God's help, all will come right in the end." At a workshop a few years ago, I invited editors and writers to rework that opening and closing as they might have been worded by any subsequent British Prime Minister, or President of the United States. The group leaped to the challenge as a starving trout leaps at a fly. The air was filled with tactical withdrawals, the need to reappraise the situation, flexible strategies, reconsolidations of previously prepared positions. In closing we were assured that the situation was well in hand, that measures were being taken to bring about the eventual resolution of all present and forthcoming difficulties. The exercise was both instructive and highly diverting. Try it with your own people.

"Water, water everywhere / Nor any drop to drink!" How would the Army Corps of Engineers have described it? "A sufficient quantity of water was available, but unfortunately none of it was suitable for human consumption." Or what would a bureaucrat do with the great line: "When two strong men stand face to face / Though they come from the ends of the earth"? He'd drop "men" like a hot rock, of course, and go into jargon about an immediate confrontation between persons of equally powerful charisma despite their highly dissimilar antecedents. . . . Have you stopped reading? Good.

The declarative sentence

The simple declarative sentence, the little word that bites—these are the tools of impact. (The declarative sentence is misdefined in many source books as "a statement of fact." Better: it's an *assertion* of fact. "The world is flat" is a declarative sentence. It's hardly a statement of fact.)

It's at least arguable that Churchill's speech before Dunkirk was what beat Hitler. It brought Britons down to the beaches to rescue their defeated army in everything from canoes to car-ferries. Talk about impact! Yet all Churchill did, all Coleridge and Kipling did in the lines quoted above, was to peel language back from the bare bones of message. Why should the rest of us find this so difficult to do? After all, it's the way we teach children to talk and write! "This is a rabbit. See the rabbit run." Impact language is easy language—easy to write, easy to read, easy to speak, easy to listen to. We *invent* the difficulties. We have to go out of our way to cumber our prose and strangle our meanings.

For maximum impact, tighten sentences around their bite-words:

Loose	Tight
The ground is covered with leaves.	Leaves cover the ground.
It was a dark night.	The night was dark.
The sky was filled with clouds.	Clouds filled the sky.

What adds to clarity and impact invariably subtracts from wordcount, an extra benefit invaluable to editors. Insurancese, the language I speak best, is infested with loose phrasing that screams to be tightened.

It is our intention to add an endorsement to this policy which will provide coverage against theft.	We intend to add theft coverage to this policy.
In order to bring about improvement in our loss ratio. . .	To improve our loss ratio. . .
It is the function of insurance to divide the risk.	The insurance function is to divide the risk.

There are countless instances. Years ago I got tired of having to look up the word "hemorrhaging" every time I had to spell it..From then until this moment I have seen no context in which "bleeding" doesn't do just as well. "In order to. . ." can always be reduced to "To. . ."; see insurancese sample above. "It might be possible" and its variants are redundancies—when you say it might, you are saying that it *is* possible. And as Professor Strunk said, or wailed, the phrase "the fact that" should be stamped on, and out.

No skill, only watchfulness, is needed for this kind of editing. It's just letting natural prose breathe naturally, prying the writer's fingers from its throat.

9

Words at work:
Persuasiveness

All letters are sales letters. Every human-to-human communication, from "I love you!" to a sign reading WET PAINT, is in some sense a sales message. The transmitters want to achieve *something,* or they wouldn't go to the trouble of writing or speaking. For the effort to succeed, some degree of agreement, cooperation, or at least response is required on the part of the receivers.

Clarity begins at home

"When all else fails," said the immortal Mr. Dooley, "a man can always fall back on honesty." We should begin and end with it. Whether we are talking to our customers, to our suppliers, to our communities, or to ourselves, we must be honest. To all readerships our job is, simply and clearly, to state facts and—when indicated—say what they mean.   When the facts are disagreeable or the news unpleasant, try for what Bergen Evans (and the *Book of Common Prayer*) has called "comfortable words." Describe problems, setbacks, new needs, matter-of-factly and even cheerfully. Never scream, never whine. Screams and whines don't sustain interest; they dull it. "This is the crisis. This is the danger. This is what has to be done about it. Let's do it!"

10

Words at work: Penetration

What makes one message or argument sink deeply in while another, equally valid, glances off and is forgotten? If I knew the answer to that fundamental question this would be a better booklet than it is, and if you know it you are wasting your time reading this section. But there are devices for barbing the prose you plant. Here are a few to keep in mind:

- **Humor.** Readers remember what makes them laugh. But humor should not be lugged in, Pat-and-Mike fashion, for its own sake. It should be, like photography or artwork, primarily *illustrative,* pertinent to and supportive of the point you are trying to make. Otherwise the joke will be remembered while the point is forgotten.

- **Pathos.** Readers also remember what makes their eyes sting. But pathos is like garlic. A very little goes a long way. Don't slobber.

- **Metaphor, simile, analogy.** Seek plain and homely figures of speech to reinforce your thought. Make them as picturesque and vivid as you can without losing the parallel.

- **Original phrasing or coinages.** These sink deeper than language which has been staled and blunted by overuse.

- **Picture words.** Movies, television, sports arenas, are making us a society of spectators. Audiences crave something to *look* at. With nothing to see but the page in front of them, readers turn their minds' eyes away from words and start to make pictures. Writers can't prevent this, but they can attempt to keep the pictures being formed in their readers' minds at least roughly in line with the prose. Language can be salted with words having fairly common, fairly predictable, visual connotations. *Apple* is a better word than fruit; *hammer* is better than tool; words like *torrent, misty, buttercup, blizzard,* incline readers to make images that advance the writer's text. Loose, empty, or abstract terms *(residence, population, statistical, vegetation, vehicle, corporation)* leave vacuums which active imaginations may fill up with images that divert readers from the writer's purpose.

- **Openings and closings.** In writing or editing, concentrate your heaviest firepower on these. The opening grabber hooks the reader into the piece; the strong closing sinks the hook.

11

Editing

What it isn't

One morning a few years before I retired, after looking
through a piece of copy, I said to its writer, "Roger, I don't
like to run footnotes at the bottom of a page."

"I do," he said.

"Oh," said I, and ran his damn footnote at the bottom
of the page.

I still agree with the commentator who said that putting
an asterisk or raised numeral in mid-page is like ringing the
reader's doorbell on the first night of his honeymoon. But it
is an established practice. There are areas in which it is not
merely your right but your duty, as editor, to substitute
your judgment for that of a contributor. Your publication
speaks for your organization, and its message must be
consistent with the organization's policies and goals. Its
voice must be clear, its language understandable. It is within
your province to follow—if you agree with them—the
suggestions set out earlier in this section.

In brief, it is a proper editorial function to iron out
wrinkles in the literacy of the prose turned in to you, always

explaining such changes to the writers and seeking their agreement. This is for the benefit not only of the publication but of the writer.

But it is a mistake to impose your own preferences and prejudices on your contributors, in areas where opinions may legitimately differ. It is not true that "everybody has a right to his own opinion"; the right to an opinion can be earned only by research and reflection. But almost everybody *thinks* he has a right to his own opinion, and if you like a quiet life you will quietly grant that right, even when it busts one or two of your own private eggs.

Explain, explain!

Your organization is made up of many departments, maybe even different companies, and each one of them has its own jargon. Each person you interview may be an expert in a particular field—physics, medicine, chemistry, accounting— but your readers will not appreciate the person or his or her expertise if they can't understand a word that's said.

Do your tactful best to persuade them to allow you to wring out the technical jargon and replace it with language your readers will understand. But if a doctor insists on calling a nosebleed a nasal hemorrhage, or a black eye *ecchymosis oculari,* swear under your breath and give way.

The Over-the-shoulder readership

Except for the tiny few who own and publish their own vehicles, every editor must please two masters. One is the nominal readership. The other is the person or people who patrols the editor's budget and salary. Unless you can satisfy both readerships, at least most of the time, you will soon find yourself asking for a transfer or reading the help-wanted ads.

Readability can suffer from the editor's effort to suit the publication to the personal tastes of the boss. Yet the boss does administer salaries. In my own corporate communications experience, I never knew a Chief Executive Officer who would argue medicine with the company's medical director, or dictate law to its lawyers. But some of them didn't hesitate to tell their editors and writers not only what to say in company publications, but how to say it.

Symptoms of this conflict are apparent in some publications. If yours is one of them, I offer this advice: tactfully but firmly assume the posture of the expert who is dealing with amateurs. Are you a one-man or one-woman editor, having to do all of your own reporting, writing, photography, and general legwork? Or have you a ten-editor staff and a degree in journalism from Columbia University? It doesn't matter. If you are paid to edit a publication, you are a professional journalist and entitled to professional status. Your president's suggestions are always welcome, and may be valuable. So are those of the switchboard operator. But all editorial decisions belong at your desk. Only a *managing* editor, with *management* recognition and responsibility, can make any publication fully readable.

12

Words with
phantom doubles

In Teutonic folklore everybody has a *doppelganger,* or
"phantom double", to confuse and make mischief for him.
Many words, or pairs of words, act as *doppelgangers* to
each other. When they are misused or misspelled, it is most
often under the shadows cast by their phantom doubles.
Here are some of these reciprocally-haunted pairings, with
suggested memory aids to distinguish the words you want
from their ghosts.

ADVERSE and AVERSE. *Adverse* means contrary or
opposed. It can describe an idea or trend or develop-
ment, never a person. *Averse* literally means turning
away, feeling distaste or repugnance. Memory said:
"My views are often *adverse* to those of my wife—but
I am anything but *averse* to her!"

AFFECT and EFFECT. To *affect* is to change,
modify, influence, or act upon. To *effect* is to
accomplish, do, make effectual. Memory aid: "To
affect is to have an *effect* upon."

APPRAISE and APPRISE. To *appraise* is to size up or evaluate. To *apprise* is to inform. Memory aid: "We have been *apprised* of your *appraisal.*"

COMPLEMENT and COMPLIMENT. To *complement* is to complete, fill in, round out. To *compliment* is to praise, commend. Memory aid: "A *complement* is a needed supplement."

COMPOSE and COMPRISE. To *compose* is to make up, form. To *comprise* is to contain, include. The whole *comprises* its parts, and is *composed* of its parts. Memory aid: "Our country *comprises* fifty different states. Fifty different states *compose* our country."

CONTINUAL and CONTINUOUS. *Continual* means frequently repeated over a period of time. *Continuous* means without any interruption at all, and may refer to either time or space. When your telephone rings *continually* you're getting a lot of calls, a *continuous* ring is one single sustained jingle. Memory aid: "The Great Wall of China runs *continuously* for 2,000 miles, and is *continually* visited by tourists."

COUNCIL and COUNSEL. A *council* is a deliberative or advisory body, convened for a particular purpose. To *counsel* is to advise, give guidance, recommend. Memory aid: "A committee of lawyers is a *council* of *counselors.*

DESPERATE and DISPARATE. *Desperate* describes a condition of extreme urgency or near hopelessness. *Disparate* means altogether unlike, sharply distinguished from. Memory aid: *"Desperate* goes with despair; *disparate* goes with disparity."

DISINTERESTED and UNINTERESTED. *Disinterested* means unbiased, not involved, having no axe to grind. *Uninterested* means indifferent, bored by the whole thing. Memory aid: "A *disinterested* witness may be greatly *interested* in a court action."

FLAUNT and FLOUT. To *flaunt* something is to display or parade it ostentatiously and usually boastfully. To *flout* is to scoff at, treat with contempt. Memory aid: "Superpatriots *flaunt* the flag; non-patriots may *flout* it."

LESS and FEWER. *Less* refers to quantity; *fewer* to number. Memory aid: "The *fewer* cows we keep, the *less* milk we'll have to drink."

NAUSEATED and NAUSEOUS. To be *nauseated* is to be driven to the point of illness by disgust or revulsion. To be *nauseous* is to be the giver of, not the sufferer from, nausea. Memory aid: "To say 'I feel *nauseous*' is to say 'I think I'm making you sick.'"

PRESCRIBE and PROSCRIBE. These are almost opposites. To *prescribe* is to establish a rule or set a course to be followed. To *proscribe* is to condemn, banish, outlaw. Memory aid: "The WCTU *prescribes proscription* of whiskey."

PRINCIPAL and PRINCIPLE. As an adjective, *principal* means most important, foremost. As a noun it means chief person or director. *Principle,* always a noun, means a basic belief or ethic, a moral guide. Memory aid: "Our school *principal* is a man of *principle.*"

RELIGIOUS and SACRILEGIOUS. No confusion of meaning here, only of spelling and pronunciation. *Sacrilegious* is commonly misspelled with an "i" in place of its "e" and mispronounced to rhyme with *religious.* Despite their surface similarity, the two words derive from entirely different sources.

SENSUAL and SENSUOUS. *Sensual* refers to the grosser physical appetites. It is a disparaging adjective. *Sensuous,* with no hint of disparagement, applies to whatever appeals to the senses. Memory aid: "*Sensuous* music need not arouse *sensual* desires." (If you had to use both words in a single sentence: "I admit I sensuous *short* letter, but at least I sensual letter.")

13

Testing—one, two, three!

Don't take these three quizzettes too seriously. They should be tackled while you and your colleagues are drinking coffee from paper cups.

One: Pluralizing the unum

The plural of reflex is reflexes. What's the plural of index? Vortex?

The plural of lackey is lackeys. What's the plural of whiskey? And of whisky (as it's spelled where the best of it comes from)?

The plural of omnibus is omnibuses. What's the plural of alumnus?

The plural of potato is potatoes. How about soprano? Hero? Zero? Embargo?

The plural of onus is onuses? What's the plural of opus?

Twice anaconda is anacondas. What about formula? Alumna? Data? (Watch it!)

The plural of jinx is jinxes. What's the plural of sphinx?

If you prophesy two or more events, you have uttered two or more—what?

Two: Pronunciamento

How does *Random House Unabridged* want you to pronounce:

acclimated	dour	machination
aggrandizement	gaol	naivete
apotheosis	hospitable	schism
clandestine	incognito	secretive
disparate	livelong	vagary

Three: Spell binding

How do you spell the six words pronounced roughly like this:

dee-SIGH-fer	HEM-O-rudge	RARE-if-eyed
DESS-i-KATE	CARE-o-SEEN	SOUP-er-SEED

That's three dozen words you have been invited to think about. If you got more than thirty of them right, you are smarter than I am and ought to be writing this section instead of reading it. Answers are on the next page—upside down if the printer will hold still for it.

Solutions

Quizzettes

ONE: Pluralizing the Unum

Singular	Doubular
index	indices
vortex	vortices
whiskey	whiskeys
whisky	whiskies
alumnus	alumna
soprano	sopranos
hero	heroes
zero	zeros or zeroes
embargo	embargoes
opus	opera
formula	formulae or formulas
alumna	alumnae
data	data *is* the plural (of datum)
sphinx	sphinges or sphinxes
prophesy (verb)	prophecy, prophecies (nouns)

TWO: Pronunciamento

ac-CLIME-ated is preferred to ACK-limated
ag-GRAND-izement (but the verb is AGG-randize)
A-POTH-e-O-sis or AP-o-THE-osis
clan-DES-teen

DIS-per-it or **dis-PAIR-it**
dour can rhyme with either "doer" or "sour"
gaol is pronounced "jail"
HOS-pitable
in-COG-nito (in-cog-NEE-to is permitted, but it's
Non-U)
livelong same as "live long"
machination is MACK-ination
naïveté is nah-EVE-tay. No options.
schism is SIZZ-um
secretive is SEE-cretive or se-CREE-tive
va-GAR-y is preferred to VAGUE-ary, especially in
British films

THREE: Spell Binding

decipher
desiccate
hemorrhage
kerosene
rarefied
supersede

Part three

Gracenotes

14

With malice
toward some

Up to now, this booklet has moved from point to point with some effort at order. The language has been temperate. The boundaries of good taste have not been breached. I have been, for me, tactful.

In this third, and from my corner of the conversation most enjoyable part, these restraints will be abandoned. So far we have been working at the job of writing and editing; now we'll be playing at it. The views offered will be at all times personal and in some cases heated. In meetings with other editors, my opinions have gotten coffee spilled and shirts torn. Tact is a sterile element at editorial conferences.

What will emerge, I hope, is something of that mysterious and indefinable quality called style, not of writing but of editing. You can make no deadlier mistake than to take your editorial direction from the prevailing practices of other media. To get the most pleasure out of your publication, the most impact into it, and the best results from it, you must develop an editorial style all your own.

The first step in that direction is a taste for joyful argument. Do you have it? Let's test it.

15

The Phony interview

Of all business media practices, the most dreadful, the most decayed, the most hotly embarrassing, the most palpably offensive to the nostrils of God, is the executive message in the form of an "interview" with the company president or Chief Executive Officer.

You know the kind of thing I mean.

Q. "Mr. Huffnpuff, how would you rate our company's performance profitwise for the year just ended?"

A. "Well, Jim, as you know, it was a very difficult year for our industry. But on balance, I think I can say. . ." and so on.

I have seen answers beginning "That's a very good question" or even "I'm glad you asked me that." In a further and equally fruitless attempt to lend credibility to the incredible, the "interview" pages are often studded with photos—Huffnpuff leaning forward, Huffnpuff leaning back, Huffnpuff frowning thoughtfully as he ponders a reply.

A genuine interview is an exchange between a questioner who doesn't know the answers and a respondent who has no control over the questions. The phony "interview" is nothing of the sort. Both questions and answers are carefully tailored to the convenience of the CEO. Indeed, no actual question-and-answer session ever takes place. It's purely a paper exercise.

To me, the most irksome aspect of the exercise is not its fraudulence but its naivete. Nobody old enough to read could for a moment be deceived by it. Successful fraud may be by general standards deplorable, but at least it has the consolations of success. What can be said for a fraud that exposes itself as it goes along?

The inverted commas around the word "interview" in this essay are sneers, inserted with the hope of persuading editors (at least) to cast executive or institutional messages as straightforward monologues. I am not trying to steer you away from fraud; it's an indispensable editorial tool. But stick to *honest* fraud.

16

Cliches:
The Sticky embrace

For several lifetimes, it was said of anything and almost everything that it was "the greatest invention since the wheel." Finally some anonymous hero, tiring of the wheel, called an innovation "the greatest invention since sliced bread." Exit wheel, enter sliced bread, and that's where the needle has stuck.

"That's how the ball bounces" has been followed by "That's how the cookie crumbles" and "That's how the mop flops." Theme and two variations: bouncing ball, crumbling cookie, flopping mop. A faint fanfare.

While you are drinking a cup of coffee you can come up with alternatives, vivid and congenial to the tongue, to all those cliches. Then why don't we do so in our writing and editing? Well, that's the insidious thing about cliches. They're habit-forming. They're sticky. We can disengage ourselves from them, but it requires effort. Which is another way of saying: we're too lazy.

Cliches do offer one plausible advantage. If they lead to lazy writing, it's *easy* writing, which makes for easy (and lazy) reading. Cliches can hardly be misunderstood, so the communication is clear. But while adding to clarity, the first ingredient in our CIPP Code, they subtract from the second element of *impact*. No phrase the reader has seen and heard hundreds of times can dent ears or dazzle eyes.

There are other drawbacks. Cliches can become encrusted in prose usage, surfacing only to fall ludicrously short of their targets. "This atom bomb—it's *dynamite*!" whispered an awe-stricken radio commentator after Hiroshima. The "mile-a-minute clip" and "going like sixty!" still occasionally pop up in an age in which everything but Congress moves faster than that.

Clash of symbols

Off-the-rack or hand-me-down language can be jarringly inappropriate, as when an oculist in a medical paper described the human eye as "something that doctors have to handle with kid gloves." And if that doesn't make your teeth chatter, only last night I heard a State Department spokesman giving the word on the Israeli-Arab confrontation. Negotiations are going smoothly, he said, but added—I could hear it coming; my stomach muscles tightened—"There are still some bugs to be ironed out."

You can *iron* out the wrinkles. You can *get* out the bugs. But anyone who talks about ironing out bugs is stuck to cliche like a fly to flypaper.

17

Sexist prose

According to every dictionary and seven centuries of prose practice, the indefinite pronouns "he", "him", and "his" mean—and mean *equally*—"she", "her", and "hers", and "man" and "mankind" include "woman" and "woman-kind." According to Ms. Ellen Cooperman, of Babylon, New York, they do not. She has had her name legally changed to "Cooperperson." (I can't help wondering what she would have done if her name had been Masterson.)

Other inroads are being made, or at least attempted. I was incredulous when informed by the head of the Affirmative Action section of the Personnel Department of my own alma mater, Wausau Insurance Companies, that I must no longer say or write "lady", "girl", or anything else but "woman" in referring to members of her sex. But sure enough, when for purposes of analogy I wrote " 'This is a good cake if I do say so myself!' croons the lady of the house" it came out to ". . .croons the baker of the cake." When I compared a grossly understated headline to "the girl who is a little bit pregnant" in a column, the editor changed "girl" to "woman." The effect in both cases was ruinous.

Bakers don't croon. The little-bit-pregnant woman is not at all the same thing as the little-bit-pregnant girl.

All sorts of questions arise. Is a little girl now a little woman? Is a newborn female child a baby woman? Are we to say "boys and women" instead of "boys and girls"? When I encounter a group of—them—do I greet them with "Good morning, women!"? (I have tried "Hi, fellas!" but have met with no very cordial response.) And if the ladies have departed, what about the gentlemen? The term "gentleman" is two words, not one, and it's the highest title any man can achieve. To earn it he must be both gentle and manly. If he lacks either quality he is no gentleman if he sits on a throne; if he possesses both he is a gentleman if he digs ditches for a living. And he deserves a matching lady.

I think feminists are wrong about this kind of thing, and it's because I am on their side that I think so. They have undeniably been made to sit below the salt since humankind came down from the trees. Women are clearly entitled to social and economic redress. But they have the semantic cart before the horse. Language doesn't create behavior; it only reflects it. It's nothing but a mirror. The behavior must be changed first, and the language enabled to follow. Breaking the mirror won't change the practice. Women are going to win their fight for equality. But they haven't won it *yet.* It's a tactical mistake for them to divert their energies from an argument they can't lose to one they not only can't win, but one that is getting them snickered at. Russell Baker's widely-quoted column, "Person the Lifeboats, the Language is Sinking!" may have set ERA back further than the whole Illinois Legislature.

Nevertheless, women *are* increasingly language-conscious, and writers and editors must take their feelings into account. Wherever masculine nouns and pronouns can be avoided without damage to prose quality, neutral terminology should be used. This doesn't mean changing every—or for that matter, any—"he" to "he or she." It can be done by pluralizing. A year ago, maybe I'd have written: "The writer should try not to put his editor on the spot." Now I'd make it: "Writers should try not to put their editors on the spot." Perhaps a second-person approach can do it: "Don't put your editor on the spot."

Rarely but occasionally, however, you will just have to choose between unsound prose and sexist prose. Only a few pages ago I found myself impaled on the bromide that "Everybody has a right to his own opinion." I worked my head to the bone trying to get that "his" out of there without collapsing the whole sentence, and couldn't do it. Can you? I know that my editors would want me to make it "Everybody has a right to *their* own opinion." They can change it if they like. I won't. I think any writer who commits singular-plural error to avoid sexist construction is out of their mind.

Prose quality comes first. Writers or editors who attempt to appease the feminists by adulterating or muddying the golden essentials of clarity, impact, persuasiveness, and penetration are guilty of the Eighth Deadly Sin.

They are trying to ride Pegasus sidesaddle.

18

Quotations: Their use and abuse

"I hate quotations!"—Ralph Waldo Emerson

The first appearance of *Bartlett's Familiar Quotations* in paperback had a swift and powerful effect on journalistic writing. With instant scholarship available for a buck and a quarter, Shakespeare and Stevenson and Shaw and the other immortals had a second coming in columns, news reports, editorials, and in the sports pages. We all wrote with *Bartlett* at our elbows. We no longer had to plough through the "Essays" to learn that Emerson hated quotations, or that he later and perhaps forgetfully said that next best to originating good lines is to be an early quoter of them, or that he triumphantly covered the contradiction by calling "a foolish consistency the hobgoblin of little minds." It's all in *Bartlett.*

But this service can be a disservice to writers and editors. It can lead them into a lazy affectation of familiarity with literature, which means away from the real thing. The best source for a quotation from Shakespeare is Shakespeare, not *Bartlett.*

"No Man—oops; Person—is an Iland, Compleat in Him/Herself, but All are a Part of the Main."
—John Donne

It's all a matter of what prompts the quotation. *Bartlett* should not be used as a literary prop. We shouldn't quote to show off. We shouldn't write articles around quotations. We shouldn't thumb through *Bartlett* to learn what other writers have said about barnacles or battleships or billygoats for ideas about what *we* can say about barnacles or battleships or billygoats. But if we know very well what we want to say, and the struggle to say it brings to mind a good and pertinent line of literature, we needn't hesitate to quote it. In short, the quotation should *follow* our thinking, not lead it.

"Timeo Danaos et dona ferentes."—some Roman

Never quote in a foreign language. If you fear the Greeks and the gifts they bring, do so in honest English. To parade Latin or French or German or whatever before an American readership is worse than pretentious snobbery—it's patronizing. The writer is deliberately going over the heads of most of the readers, and saying "I am an intellectual addressing other intellectuals. You lowbrows can go stuff yourselves." This offends not just the lowbrows, but the truly intelligent.

Can you remember the "Fractured French" fad that swept the campuses back in the fifties? *La meme chose* translated to "Your fly is open." *Tant pis* meant "Nurse, I need the catheter." Like all fads it was short-lived, but while it endured it was a deadly deflater. If a speaker attempted to grace a lecture with a line in a foreign tongue, a dozen sepulchral voices from the back of the room would murmur "Louis sank." The fad didn't last long, but for some of us the lesson did. To quote again: if English was good enough for Jesus Christ, it's good enough for you and me.

19

Short turns
and encores

Time off for bad behavior

All writers, and writing editors, worth their salt are born
vacillators. This is because we have less control over our
imaginations than normal people. Compelled to deal with a
specific topic, we will instinctively and immediately think
about something else, anything else, *everything* else. I can't
prove it, but I choose to believe that Shakespeare wrote
"The Merry Wives of Windsor" when he was *supposed* to
be writing "Henry the Fifth." He was sick and tired of all
those Henrys. Oh, sure, he got around to "Henry the Fifth"
eventually, and the rest of us get around to our appointed
tasks eventually, but not before taking a few healing
moments for therapeutic vacillation. The following
reflections emerged from such intervals of bad behavior.

From doctorfish to skimble-skamble

Do you know what a *doctorfish* is? Or *izzat*? Or *turpeth*? Or a *rundle*? Or whether you play, wear, or eat a *shofar*? Or who *Tancred* was?

You very likely do if your dictionary is *Random House Unabridged*. These are all guide words above its columns. Other esoterica include *podesta, keet, coehorn, wyvern, skimble-skamble*. Flaunt words like these in boldface before normally healthy writers, and no matter how urgent their proper errands to the dictionary may be, they will dive after them. If yours is another dictionary, of course, you probably have a different set of your own.

Practical communication value of these exotic terms, it must be admitted, is uncertain. Dropped casually into conversation, they can sometimes produce a stunned silence. But only sometimes. A lady at a cocktail party asked me why pork is offensive to Hindu diets. "Matter of izzat," I said, negligently flicking a speck of avocado dip from my sleeve. "Do you use the *Random House Unabridged Dictionary*?" she asked brightly. Win some, lose some.

Good and well

Let's quit saying "I feel well" when we mean "I feel *good*" and "I feel badly" when we mean "I feel *bad*." Adjectives, not adverbs, are wanted here. We don't say "I feel warmly" or "I feel hopefully" or "I feel finely", do we? To say "I feel well" is just flatly and unarguably to be guilty of defective grammar, unless you mean "I manipulate my tactile and sensory apparatus with discrimination and adroitness."

The Wandering only

No other modifier drifts so frequently or so far from its moorings as the word *only.* "You only can buy Allstate insurance from an Allstate agent," reads an advertisement by that great company. This could mean that only *you,* nobody else, can buy the insurance. It could mean that you can only *buy* it, not borrow it or steal it or get it for nothing. It could mean that you can buy only *insurance,* not candy bars or canoes or cattle prods, from the agent. It could even mean what it's intended to mean—that only an Allstate agent can sell you Allstate insurance—but that's about as far as a modifier can get from its modifyee.

Got damned

The verb "got," to denote possession, is in disrepute. Some grammarians would wash it out of usage altogether, and—for grammarians—they are not far from right. "I have" is generally neater than "I've got." But it's also less emphatic. "Why don't you get a dog?" "I have a dog." "Oh, sure, but why don't you get a *good* dog?" "I've *got* a good dog!" Anybody who would tamely repeat "have" in that context doesn't *deserve* a good dog.

Hobson's choice

In reading through stacks of articles and speeches, I have hardly ever seen this term used properly. A "Hobson's choice" is a choice, not between or among equally distasteful alternatives or options, but between one thing and nothing at all. Hobson was a liveryman with saddle horses for hire. But the customer had to accept the horse nearest the stable door or go horseless. Thus *Hobson's choice* denotes (for instance) not a menu listing several things, none of which you like, but one offering only one thing whether you like it or not.

Gallicism

As everybody knows, to summon a waiter in a French restaurant one utters the word "Garcon!" But *garcon* means boy. What's the sang-froid for waitress? My brother, a passionate Francophile, assures me that the feminine equivalent of "Garcon!" is "Bun!"—an idiom for *bonne,* itself a contraction of *bonne femme.* This is a classic case of knowledge for its own sake. No restaurant of my acquaintance is sophisticated enough for the word, making this paragraph the first place I have ever been able to use it.

Sparkling dialogue

Eleanor Farjeon, the gifted British author of *Martin Pippin in the Apple Orchard* and other children's books, employs a crisp, clear, and beautifully economic device for multiple dialogue that deserves attention and emulation. It works like this:

	"Yes,"		Julie.
	"No,"		Marjorie.
	"Maybe,"		Gavin.
"Is it time?" asked	"I think so,"	} answered {	Timothy.
Martin.	"I doubt it,"		James.
	"Of course,"		Jennifer.
	"Certainly not!"		Robin.

The lively impression of everybody talking at once brings to the printed page some of the qualities of a graphic.

Clock watching

Over martinis, I will undertake to demonstrate that the nominal opposites *clockwise* and *counter-clockwise* are in fact synonymous. *Clockwise* means in the wise—i.e.: the way—of a clock. To do anything clockwise means to do it the way a clock does. Okay, you're a clock. Your face is the clock's face; your hands are the clock's hands. Now, if you'll move your hands the way a clock does, you'll be moving them counter-clockwise.

At this point some pundit, probably drinking scotch and ginger ale, will object that this is only from the clock's viewpoint. "When we say 'clockwise' we mean from *our* point of view." But when we refer to the right arm of a chair, the left wing of a house, the starboard rail of a ship, we are taking the viewpoint of the chair or the house or the ship. We owe a like courtesy to clocks. They have more personality than some people.

Exception overruled

"There is an exception to every rule," runs the ancient axiom. But wait a minute. The axiom itself *states* a rule. If there is an exception to every rule, there has to be an exception to the rule that there is an exception to every rule—which makes hash of the axiom.

One-way message

In one of his books, Stuart Chase says that there is no such thing as a clear and effective one-way communication; that unless there is a received and understood response, the message must be deemed to have failed of its purpose.

Effective one-way communication is certainly rare, but it

can occur. I asked a friend who is totally color-blind if there were any way he could make that condition comprehensible to me. "It's very simple," he said. "You see a difference between color film and black-and-white film. They look exactly the same to me, and that's the way I see life." This indeed put me right into his picture. Then he said, a little wistfully, "Now, *you* tell *me* what it's like to see colors." And there communication ceased. Clear, effective, one-way.

Maybe I worry too much about this kind of thing

"As far as any improvement in the economic picture, at least before next spring, the prospects remain very dim." This lapse—omission of the needed ". . . goes" or ". . . is concerned"—is nearly always oral. We seldom see it in print. Another common speech remission is "I could care less" when the speaker obviously means that he *couldn't* care less.

Then there's the person who is eating peanuts (or whatever) "like they're going out of style." But the one sure thing about anything going out of style is that desire for it is diminishing, not increasing. To use or do something "like it's going out of style" ought to mean using or doing it less and less, not more and more.

Stowaways

It's odd how some words pick up stowaway syllables much as boats pick up barnacles, and with like effect on the seaworthiness of the vessels. Examples: "reoccurrence" for *recurrence,* "disassociate" for *dissociate,* "preventative" for *preventive.* To "orientate" is the unEnglish for *to orient,* but probably this one derived backward from "orientation"— which should have been *or-ention* in the first place.

Instant nuptials

A Wausau (Wisconsin) couple has been refused permission to be married via long-distance telephone by the bride's father, a minister living abroad. The Wausau *Daily Herald* quotes the County Clerk as ruling that under the law, "the ceremony must be consummated before a duly authorized officiating person and at least two competent adult witnesses."

Your turn

I dislike and distrust questionnaires. They are usually highly defective efforts at communication. But if you'll complete and return this one, on the following page, I promise you a personal, thoughtful, and, if indicated, heated reply.

....

QUESTIONNAIRE

Digby Butler Whitman
3440 Riverview Court
Wausau, Wisconsin 54401

Dear Digby:

This is what I think.